General Knowledge

1) Who was the team's top-scorer in the Championship during the 2007/08 season with 22 goals?

2) Which long-serving player made his debut against Norwich in October 2000 after coming through the Sheffield United youth system?

3) What number shirt has Chris Basham worn since he joined the club in 2014?

4) Who became the first Zimbabwean to represent the club after he signed in 2001?

5) Who became permanent club captain in 2011?

6) Who became the clubs youngest ever player when he appeared off the bench in a League One game versus Rotherham in April 2014?

7) Which player broke the record for the youngest ever Sheffield United goal-scorer when he netted against Grimsby in the EFL Trophy in 2016?

8) Who scored Sheffield United's first goal of the 21st Century, during a 2-2 draw away to Grimsby on the 3rd of January?

9) Phil Jagielka scored an own goal to see United lose 2-1 away to which side in April 2021?

10) United drew 0-0 at home to which side in September 2006, after Paddy Kenny saved a penalty and the Blades missed two spot-kicks of their own?

11) Who scored a hat-trick in the 3-0 away win at Gillingham in January 2004?

12) Which company was the main shirt sponsor for the 2006/07 season in the Premier League?

13) Who finished the game in goal in the 1-0 win over Arsenal in December 2006?

14) The Blades were controversially denied a goal versus Aston Villa in June 2020 when the goal-line technology failed to show that a free-kick from which player had been carried over the line?

15) Which Burnley player scored the winner in the 2009 Championship Play-Off final?

16) United lost out to Swindon in the League One Play-Off semi-final in 2015 by what aggregate score?

17) Promotion from League One was confirmed in April 2017 after a 2-1 win away against which side?

18) United conceded a last-minute equaliser to draw 1-1 at home to which team being managed by Neil Warnock in April 2018?

19) Which former United player scored against them on the final day of the Premier League season to see Wigan win 2-1 and relegate the Blades in 2007?

20) By what score did Wolves win the First Division Play-Off final in 2003?

21) Who missed the final penalty as United lost an extraordinary League One Play-Off final shoot-out 8-7 to Huddersfield in 2012?

22) United suffered yet more Play-Off heartache when they lost in the semi-finals to which club in 2013?

23) How many points did Sheffield United end the season with when winning the League One title in the 2016/17 season?

24) Who scored the winner as the club claimed their first win back in the Premier League, against Crystal Palace in August 2019?

25) The Blades finally won their first game of the 2020/2021 Premier League season after 18 attempts by beating Newcastle, but which two clubs had United drawn with up to that stage?

Transfers 2000-2009

1) From which club did Sheffield United sign Michael Brown in January 2000?

2) Who was Shaun Derry sold to in March 2000?

3) Which striker was sold to Blackburn in November 2000?

4) From which club did Peter Ndlovu arrive in February 2001?

5) Which striker was purchased from Fulham in July 2001?

6) Who did Gus Uhlenbeek sign for from United in August 2002?

7) Which central midfielder signed from Bradford City in July 2002?

8) Which goalkeeper arrived from Bury in October 2002?

9) From which side was Dean Windass signed in January 2003?

10) From which club did Chris Morgan join in July 2003?

11) Which team signed Michael Brown in January 2004?

12) Which two players signed from Sheffield Wednesday in June 2004?

13) Which forward arrived from Watford in June 2005?

14) Which striker left to join Millwall in August 2004?

15) Who was sold to Scunthorpe in August 2005?

16) From which club did Keith Gillespie arrive on a free transfer in August 2005?

17) Which striker was brought in from Burnley in January 2006?

18) Which goalkeeper came in from Leeds United in August 2006?

19) Which defender was bought from Everton in July 2007?

20) David Unsworth left in the January 2007 transfer window to sign for which team?

21) Claude Davis was sold to which side in July 2007?

22) From which club did United sign Ugo Ehiogu in January 2008?

23) Which player was sold to Valerenga in July 2008?

24) Which striker did United buy from Watford in July 2008?

25) Tottenham bought which two Sheffield United players in July 2009?

26) Which player signed for the club from Watford in July 2009?

Cup Games

1) Which two players missed their penalties as United lost to Arsenal in the FA Cup Fifth Round in 2005?

2) Which team did the Blades beat on penalties in the Football League Trophy first round in 2015?

3) What was the final score in the FA Cup Semi-Final loss to Hull city in 2014?

4) In which season did United reach the Semi-Final of both the FA and League Cups?

5) Who scored the only goal to knock Leeds United out of the FA Cup at the Quarter-Final stage in 2003?

6) Which Premier League team did Sheffield United knock out of the FA Cup at the Third Round stage in 2014?

7) Which non-league team did United beat 2-1 in the FA Cup Third Round in 2020?

8) Who scored the only goal in the 1-0 victory over Bristol City in the 2021 FA Cup Fifth Round?

9) Who scored a hat-trick as Leyton Orient were beaten 6-0 in the FA Cup First Round in November 2016?

10) By what score did Arsenal will the Third Round League Cup tie in 2008?

11) Which Spurs player scored late on to seal a 3-2 aggregate win in the League Cup Semi-Final of 2015?

12) United had earned their place in that Semi-Final after beating Southampton 1-0 in the previous round, but who scored the winner against the Saints?

Memorable Games

1) What was the result in the 100th Steel City derby, played at Hillsborough in April 2001?

2) Who scored the only goal as United recorded their first Premier League win of the season against Newcastle in January 2021?

3) Which team did the Blade beat 5-3 at home in League One in September 2012?

4) Who scored the only goal as Arsenal were beaten at Bramall Lane in the Premier League in December 2006?

5) By what score-line did United beat Sheffield Wednesday away from home in September 2017?

6) Which Sheffield United player netted the winner as the Blades won 2-1 at Old Trafford in January 2021?

7) In the 2018/2019 Championship season, both Sheffield derby games ended in what result?

8) Who scored a penalty in the Steel City derby in December 2000, only to see Wednesday equalise to claim a 1-1 draw at Bramall Lane?

9) United beat which already relegated team 2-0 at home in late April 2019 to effectively seal their promotion to the Premier League?

10) Which team were beaten 4-1 at Bramall Lane in the opening game of the 2005/2006 Championship season?

11) Sheffield United lost a remarkable game to Fulham in November 2017 by what score?

12) Who scored the stoppage time winner
    as United beat Wolves 1-0 in July 2020?

Memorable Goals

1) Who scored the winner with a beautiful volley from the edge of the box against Charlton in December 2006?

2) Who was the unlikely scorer with an acrobatic scissor kick away to Nottingham Forest in the FA Cup in January 2004?

3) Phil Jagielka hit a sensational long-range volley to secure a last-minute win against which team in September 2006?

4) Jagielka had also scored a remarkably similar goal to help knock which team out of the League Cup in November 2002?

5) Who scored from near the touch-line after Bolton goalkeeper Jussi Jaaskelainen left his goal-mouth to make a clearance in November 2006?

6) Who scored with an incredible solo effort in the dying seconds of the game as United lost in the League One Play-Offs to Swindon Town in 2015?

7) Which player nearly took the net off with a powerfully struck free-kick against West Ham in April 2007?

8) Who scored the last equaliser in United's first game back in the Premier League, away to Bournemouth in August 2019?

9) David McGoldrick scored his first Premier League goals during the 3-0 win over which team in July 2020?

10) Who scored the crucial winner away to Leeds in March 2019?

Red Cards

1) Who was sent off alongside Millwall's Kevin Muscat after an incident between the two at half-time in the meeting between the sides in December 2004?

2) Which three Sheffield United players were sent off in the now infamous 'Battle of Bramall Lane' against West Brom in 2002?

3) Keith Gillespie was sent off 10 seconds after coming on as a substitute against which team in January 2007?

4) Who was sent off in the Premier League 1-1 draw away to Brighton in December 2020?

5) Which Arsenal player was sent off during the 1-1 draw in their FA Cup tie in February 2005?

6) Who was sent off for violent conduct late on in the 2-2 home draw with Millwall in November 2005?

7) The Blades lost 1-0 to Sheffield Wednesday in October 2008 despite seeing which opposing player dismissed inside the first half an hour?

8) Which two players were dismissed as nine-man United lost 3-0 away to Watford in March 2011?

9) Which defender was harshly sent off for a foul on Andy Johnson in the loss to Everton in October 2006?

10) In the match against Brentford in April 2014, which Blades player was initially sent off, before the referee rescinded his decision?

11) United fought back to earn a 2-2 draw against which side in February 2015, having seen Jose Baxter dismissed early on?

12) Which Sheffield United player became the first to have a red card overturned in the match with Norwich in 2019?

13) Who saw red in the 2-1 home defeat to Bristol City in December 2017?

Managers

1) Who was the Sheffield United manager at the beginning of the 21st Century?

2) Which team did United face in their last game under the management of Neil Warnock?

3) For how many matches did David Weir take charge of the club?

4) Nigel Adkins took over as manager from who in 2015?

5) What was the result in Chris Wilder's first game as Sheffield United manager?

6) Which manager was unable to stop the team from being relegated to League One in 2011?

7) Who was in charge as United lost in the 2014/15 Play-Offs to Swindon?

8) Which club did Nigel Adkins lose to in his final game as manager?

9) Which manager re-signed Billy Sharp for the club in 2015?

10) How many games did Micky Adams win out of his 24 games in charge?

First Goals

Can you name the club that these players scored their first goal for Sheffield United against?

1) Phil Jagielka

2) Paul Peschisolido

3) Dean Windass

4) Chris Morgan

5) Danny Webber

6) Billy Sharp

7) Jon Stead

8) James Beattie

9) Harry Maguire

10) Chris Basham

11) Che Adams

12) Leon Clarke

13) John Lundstram

14) David McGoldrick

15) Oli McBurnie

16) Sander Berge

17) Oliver Burke

18) Kean Bryan

Transfers 2010-2021

1) Which central defender left to join Sunderland in January 2010?

2) United signed which goalkeeper on a free from Stoke City in July 2010?

3) Which midfielder joined from Swansea in August 2010, only to be sold back to Swansea in January 2011?

4) Which two players left to join Charlton in the summer of 2010?

5) Ryan Flynn was signed from which club in July 2011?

6) Which young player was sold to Blackburn in August 2011?

7) Who did United sign from Middlesbrough in July 2012?

8) Which defender was sold to Aston Villa in July 2012?

9) From which club was Barry Robson signed in January 2013?

10) Which forward arrived from Walsall in June 2013?

11) Striker Dave Kitson left to join which club in June 2013?

12) To which side was forward Lyle Taylor sold in June 2014?

13) Which defender was sold to Hull City in July 2014?

14) Which winger arrived from Rochdale in February 2015?

15) Midfielder Dean Hammond signed on a free after leaving which team in July 2016?

16) Who joined United from Coventry on a free in July 2016?

17) Who did James McEveley sign for on a free transfer in June 2016?

18) Which young striker left United to sign for Everton in July 2016?

19) Who was sold to Birmingham in the summer of 2016?

20) Which goalkeeper was sold to Bournemouth in January 2017?

21) From which club was Leon Clarke bought in July 2016?

22) John Lundstram came in from which side in 2017?

23) Which forward was signed from QPR in August 2018?

24) From which club did United sign Sander Berge in the 2020 January transfer window?

25) Who did Ravel Morrison sign for after leaving in the summer of 2020?

26) Which two players arrived from Derby County in September 2020?

Answers

General Knowledge Answers

1) Who was the team's top-scorer in the Championship during the 2007/08 season with 22 goals?
James Beattie

2) Which long-serving player made his debut against Norwich in October 2000 after coming through the Sheffield United youth system?
Nick Montgomery

3) What number shirt has Chris Basham worn since he joined the club in 2014?
6

4) Who became the first Zimbabwean to represent the club after he signed in 2001?
Peter Ndlovu

5) Who became permanent club captain in 2011?
Michael Doyle

6) Who became the clubs youngest ever player when he appeared off the bench in a League One game versus Rotherham in April 2014?
Louis Reed

7) Which player broke the record for the youngest ever Sheffield United goal-scorer when he netted against Grimsby in the EFL Trophy in 2016?
Regan Slater

8) Who scored Sheffield United's first goal of the 21st Century, during a 2-2 draw away to Grimsby on the 3rd of January?
Marcus Bent

9) Phil Jagielka scored an own goal to see United lose 2-1 away to which side in April 2021?
Leeds United

10) United drew 0-0 at home to which side in September 2006, after Paddy Kenny saved a penalty and the Blades missed two spot-kicks of their own?
Blackburn Rovers

11) Who scored a hat-trick in the 3-0 away win at Gillingham in January 2004?
Paul Peschisolido

12) Which company was the main shirt sponsor for the 2006/07 season in the Premier League?
Capital One

13) Who finished the game in goal in the 1-0 win over Arsenal in December 2006?
Phil Jagielka

14) The Blades were controversially denied a goal versus Aston Villa in June 2020 when the goal-line technology failed to show that a free-kick from which player had been carried over the line?
Oliver Norwood

15) Which Burnley player scored the winner in the 2009 Championship Play-Off final?
Wade Elliott

16) United lost out to Swindon in the League One Play-Off semi-final in 2015 by what aggregate score?
Swindon 7-6 Sheffield United

17) Promotion from League One was confirmed in April 2017 after a 2-1 win away against which side?
Northampton Town

18) United conceded a last-minute equaliser to draw 1-1 at home to which team being managed by Neil Warnock in April 2018?
Cardiff City

19) Which former United player scored against them on the final day of the Premier League season to see Wigan win 2-1 and relegate the Blades in 2007?
David Unsworth

20) By what score did Wolves win the First Division Play-Off final in 2003?
Sheffield United 0-3 Wolverhampton

21) Who missed the final penalty as United lost an extraordinary League One Play-Off final shoot-out 8-7 to Huddersfield in 2012?
Steve Simonsen

22) United suffered yet more Play-Off heartache when they lost in the semi-finals to which club in 2013?
Yeovil

23) How many points did Sheffield United end the season with when winning the League One title in the 2016/17 season?
100

24) Who scored the winner as the club claimed their first win back in the Premier League, against Crystal Palace in August 2019?
John Lundstram

25) The Blades finally won their first game of the 2020/2021 Premier League season after 18 attempts by beating Newcastle, but which two clubs had United drawn with up to that stage?

Fulham and Brighton

Transfers 2000-2009 Answers

1) From which club did Sheffield United sign Michael Brown in January 2000?
Manchester City

2) Who was Shaun Derry sold to in March 2000?
Portsmouth

3) Which striker was sold to Blackburn in November 2000?
Marcus Bent

4) From which club did Peter Ndlovu arrive in February 2001?
Birmingham City

5) Which striker was purchased from Fulham in July 2001?
Paul Peschisolido

6) Who did Gus Uhlenbeek sign for from United in August 2002?
Bradford City

7) Which central midfielder signed from Bradford City in July 2002?
Stuart McCall

8) Which goalkeeper arrived from Bury in October 2002?
Paddy Kenny

9) From which side was Dean Windass signed in January 2003?
Middlesbrough

10) From which club did Chris Morgan join in July 2003?
Barnsley

11) Which team signed Michael Brown in January 2004?
Tottenham Hotspur

12) Which two players signed from Sheffield Wednesday in June 2004?
Alan Quinn and Leigh Bromby

13) Which forward arrived from Watford in June 2005?

Danny Webber

14) Which striker left to join Millwall in August 2004?

Barry Hayles

15) Who was sold to Scunthorpe in August 2005?

Billy Sharp

16) From which club did Keith Gillespie arrive on a free transfer in August 2005?

Leicester City

17) Which striker was brought in from Burnley in January 2006?

Ade Akinbiyi

18) Which goalkeeper came in from Leeds United in August 2006?

Ian Bennett

19) Which defender was bought from Everton in July 2007?
Gary Naysmith

20) David Unsworth left in the January 2007 transfer window to sign for which team?
Wigan

21) Claude Davis was sold to which side in July 2007?
Derby County

22) From which club did United sign Ugo Ehiogu in January 2008?
Rangers

23) Which player was sold to Valerenga in July 2008?
Luton Shelton

24) Which striker did United buy from Watford in July 2008?
Darius Henderson

25) Tottenham bought which two Sheffield United players in July 2009?
Kyle Naughton and Kyle Walker

26) Which player signed for the club from Watford in July 2009?
Leigh Bromby

Cup Games Answers

1) Which two players missed their penalties as United lost to Arsenal in the FA Cup Fifth Round in 2005?
Alan Quinn and Jon Harley

2) Which team did the Blades beat on penalties in the Football League Trophy first round in 2015?
Hartlepool

3) What was the final score in the FA Cup Semi-Final loss to Hull city in 2014?
5-3

4) In which season did United reach the Semi-Final of both the FA and League Cups?
2002/03

5) Who scored the only goal to knock Leeds United out of the FA Cup at the Quarter-Final stage in 2003?
Steve Kabba

6) Which Premier League team did Sheffield United knock out of the FA Cup at the Third Round stage in 2014?
Aston Villa

7) Which non-league team did United beat 2-1 in the FA Cup Third Round in 2020?
AFC Fylde

8) Who scored the only goal in the 1-0 victory over Bristol City in the 2021 FA Cup Fifth Round?
Billy Sharp

9) Who scored a hat-trick as Leyton Orient were beaten 6-0 in the FA Cup First Round in November 2016?
Harry Chapman

10) By what score did Arsenal will the Third Round League Cup tie in 2008?
6-0

11) Which Spurs player scored late on to seal a 3-2 aggregate win in the League Cup Semi-Final of 2015?
Christian Eriksen

12) United had earned their place in that Semi-Final after beating Southampton 1-0 in the previous round, but who scored the winner against the Saints?
Marc McNulty

Memorable Games Answers

1) What was the result in the 100th Steel City derby, played at Hillsborough in April 2001?
Sheffield Wednesday 1-2 Sheffield United

2) Who scored the only goal as United recorded their first Premier League win of the season against Newcastle in January 2021?
Billy Sharp

3) Which team did the Blade beat 5-3 at home in League One in September 2012?
Bournemouth

4) Who scored the only goal as Arsenal were beaten at Bramall Lane in the Premier League in December 2006?
Christian Nade

5) By what score-line did United beat Sheffield Wednesday away from home in September 2017?
Sheffield Wednesday 2-4 Sheffield United

6) Which Sheffield United player netted the winner as the Blades won 2-1 at Old Trafford in January 2021?
Oliver Burke

7) In the 2018/2019 Championship season, both Sheffield derby games ended in what result?
0-0

8) Who scored a penalty in the Steel City derby in December 2000, only to see Wednesday equalise to claim a 1-1 draw at Bramall Lane?
Bobby Ford

9) United beat which already relegated team 2-0 at home in late April 2019 to effectively seal their promotion to the Premier League?

Ipswich Town

10) Which team were beaten 4-1 at Bramall Lane in the opening game of the 2005/2006 Championship season?

Leicester City

11) Sheffield United lost a remarkable game to Fulham in November 2017 by what score?

Sheffield United 4-5 Fulham

12) Who scored the stoppage time winner as United beat Wolves 1-0 in July 2020?

John Egan

Memorable Goals Answers

1) Who scored the winner with a beautiful volley from the edge of the box against Charlton in December 2006?
Keith Gillespie

2) Who was the unlikely scorer with an acrobatic scissor kick away to Nottingham Forest in the FA Cup in January 2004?
Chris Morgan

3) Phil Jagielka hit a sensational long-range volley to secure a last-minute win against which team in September 2006?
Middlesbrough

4) Jagielka had also scored a remarkably similar goal to help knock which team out of the League Cup in November 2002?
Leeds United

5) Who scored from near the touch-line after Bolton goalkeeper Jussi Jaaskelainen left his goal-mouth to make a clearance in November 2006?
Colin Kazim-Richards

6) Who scored with an incredible solo effort in the dying seconds of the game as United lost in the League One Play-Offs to Swindon Town in 2015?
Che Adams

7) Which player nearly took the net off with a powerfully struck free-kick against West Ham in April 2007?
Michael Tonge

8) Who scored the last equaliser in United's first game back in the Premier League, away to Bournemouth in August 2019?
Billy Sharp

9) David McGoldrick scored his first Premier League goals during the 3-0 win over which team in July 2020?
Chelsea

10) Who scored the crucial winner away to Leeds in March 2019?
Chris Basham

Red Cards Answers

1) Who was sent off alongside Millwall's Kevin Muscat after an incident between the two at half-time in the meeting between the sides in December 2004?
Paddy Kenny

2) Which three Sheffield United players were sent off in the now infamous 'Battle of Bramall Lane' against West Brom in 2002?
Simon Tracey, Patrick Suffo and Georges Santos

3) Keith Gillespie was sent off 10 seconds after coming on as a substitute against which team in January 2007?
Reading

4) Who was sent off in the Premier League 1-1 draw away to Brighton in December 2020?
John Lundstram

5) Which Arsenal player was sent off during the 1-1 draw in their FA Cup tie in February 2005?
Dennis Bergkamp

6) Who was sent off for violent conduct late on in the 2-2 home draw with Millwall in November 2005?
Chris Morgan

7) The Blades lost 1-0 to Sheffield Wednesday in October 2008 despite seeing which opposing player dismissed inside the first half an hour?
Matt Kilgallon

8) Which two players were dismissed as nine-man United lost 3-0 away to Watford in March 2011?
Darius Henderson and Lee Williamson

9) Which defender was harshly sent off for a foul on Andy Johnson in the loss to Everton in October 2006?
Claude Davis

10) In the match against Brentford in April 2014, which Blades player was initially sent off, before the referee rescinded his decision?

Kieron Freeman

11) United fought back to earn a 2-2 draw against which side in February 2015, having seen Jose Baxter dismissed early on?

Coventry City

12) Which Sheffield United player became the first to have a red card overturned in the match with Norwich in 2019?

Chris Basham

13) Who saw red in the 2-1 home defeat to Bristol City in December 2017?

John Fleck

Managers Answers

1) Who was the Sheffield United manager at the beginning of the 21st Century?
Neil Warnock

2) Which team did United face in their last game under the management of Neil Warnock?
Wigan

3) For how many matches did David Weir take charge of the club?
13

4) Nigel Adkins took over as manager from who in 2015?
Nigel Clough

5) What was the result in Chris Wilder's first game as Sheffield United manager?
Bolton 1-0 Sheffield United

6) Which manager was unable to stop the team from being relegated to League One in 2011?
Micky Adams

7) Who was in charge as United lost in the 2014/15 Play-Offs to Swindon?
Nigel Clough

8) Which club did Nigel Adkins lose to in his final game as manager?
Scunthorpe

9) Which manager re-signed Billy Sharp for the club in 2015?
Nigel Adkins

10) How many games did Micky Adams win out of his 24 games in charge?
Four

First Goals Answers

1) Phil Jagielka
   Burnley

2) Paul Peschisolido
   Birmingham City

3) Dean Windass
   Bradford City

4) Chris Morgan
   Bradford City

5) Danny Webber
   Leeds United

6) Billy Sharp
   Morecambe

7) Jon Stead
   Fulham

8) James Beattie
   Colchester United

9) Harry Maguire
   Oldham Athletic

10) Chris Basham
   Swindon Town

11) Che Adams
   Tottenham Hotspur

12) Leon Clarke
   Crewe Alexandra

13) John Lundstram
   Nottingham Forest

14) David McGoldrick
   QPR

15) Oli McBurnie
   Leicester City

16) Sander Berge
   Tottenham Hotspur

17) Oliver Burke
Bristol Rovers

18) Kean Bryan
Manchester United

Transfers 2010-2021 Answers

1) Which central defender left to join Sunderland in January 2010?
Matt Kilgallon

2) United signed which goalkeeper on a free from Stoke City in July 2010?
Steve Simonsen

3) Which midfielder joined from Swansea in August 2010, only to be sold back to Swansea in January 2011?
Leon Britton

4) Which two players left to join Charlton in the summer of 2010?
Kyel Reid and Jonathan Fortune

5) Ryan Flynn was signed from which club in July 2011?
Falkirk

6) Which young player was sold to Blackburn in August 2011?
Jordan Slew

7) Who did United sign from Middlesbrough in July 2012?
Tony McMahon

8) Which defender was sold to Aston Villa in July 2012?
Matthew Lowton

9) From which club was Barry Robson signed in January 2013?
Vancouver Whitecaps

10) Which forward arrived from Walsall in June 2013?
Febian Brandy

11) Striker Dave Kitson left to join which club in June 2013?
Oxford United

12) To which side was forward Lyle Taylor sold in June 2014?
Scunthorpe

13) Which defender was sold to Hull City in July 2014?
Harry Maguire

14) Which winger arrived from Rochdale in February 2015?
Matt Done

15) Midfielder Dean Hammond signed on a free after leaving which team in July 2016?
Leicester City

16) Who joined United from Coventry on a free in July 2016?
John Fleck

17) Who did James McEveley sign for on a free transfer in June 2016?
Ross County

18) Which young striker left United to sign for Everton in July 2016?
Dominic Calvert-Lewin

19) Who was sold to Birmingham in the summer of 2016?
Che Adams

20) Which goalkeeper was sold to Bournemouth in January 2017?
Aaron Ramsdale

21) From which club was Leon Clarke bought in July 2016?
Bury

22) John Lundstram came in from which side in 2017?
Oxford United

23) Which forward was signed from QPR in August 2018?
Conor Washington

24) From which club did United sign Sander Berge in the 2020 January transfer window?
Genk

25) Who did Ravel Morrison sign for after leaving in the summer of 2020?
Den Haag

26) Which two players arrived from Derby County in September 2020?
Max Lowe and Jayden Bogle

If you enjoyed this book please consider leaving a five star review on Amazon

Books by Jack Pearson available on Amazon:

Cricket:

Cricket World Cup 2019 Quiz Book
The Ashes 2019 Cricket Quiz Book
The Ashes 2010-2019 Quiz Book
The Ashes 2005 Quiz Book
The Indian Premier League Quiz Book

Football:

The Quiz Book of the England Football Team in the 21st Century
The Quiz Book of Arsenal Football Club in the 21st Century
The Quiz Book of Aston Villa Football Club in the 21st Century
The Quiz Book of Chelsea Football Club in the 21st Century

The Quiz Book of Everton Football Club in the 21st Century

The Quiz Book of Leeds United Football Club in the 21st Century

The Quiz Book of Leicester City Football Club in the 21st Century

The Quiz Book of Liverpool Football Club in the 21st Century

The Quiz Book of Manchester City Football Club in the 21st Century

The Quiz Book of Manchester United Football Club in the 21st Century

The Quiz Book of Newcastle United Football Club in the 21st Century

The Quiz Book of Southampton Football Club in the 21st Century

The Quiz Book of Sunderland Association Football Club in the 21st Century

The Quiz Book of Tottenham Hotspur Football Club in the 21st Century

The Quiz Book of West Ham United Football Club in the 21st Century

The Quiz Book of Wrexham Association Football Club in the 21st Century

Printed in Great Britain
by Amazon

81791876R00037